Greater Than a Tourist Book Series
Reviews from Readers

I think the series is wonderful and beneficial for tourists to get information before visiting the city.

-Seckin Zumbul, Izmir Turkey

I am a world traveler who has read many trip guides but this one really made a difference for me. I would call it a heartfelt creation of a local guide expert instead of just a guide.

-Susy, Isla Holbox, Mexico

New to the area like me, this is a must have!

 -Joe, Bloomington, USA

This is a good series that gets down to it when looking for things to do at your destination without having to read a novel for just a few ideas.

-Rachel, Monterey, USA

Good information to have to plan my trip to this destination.

-Pennie Farrell, Mexico

Great ideas for a port day.
-Mary Martin USA

Aptly titled, you won't just be a tourist after reading this book. You'll be greater than a tourist!
-Alan Warner, Grand Rapids, USA

Even though I only have three days to spend in San Miguel in an upcoming visit, I will use the author's suggestions to guide some of my time there. An easy read - with chapters named to guide me in directions I want to go.
-Robert Catapano, USA

Great insights from a local perspective! Useful information and a very good value!
-Sarah, USA

This series provides an in-depth experience through the eyes of a local. Reading these series will help you to travel the city in with confidence and it'll make your journey a unique one.
-Andrew Teoh, Ipoh, Malaysia

GREATER THAN A TOURIST- SALEM MASSACHUSETTS USA

50 Travel Tips from a Local

Danielle Lasher

Cover designed by: Ivana Stamenkovic
Cover Image: https://pixabay.com/photos/house-of-seven-gables-salem-404200/

CZYK Publishing Since 2011.

Greater Than a Tourist

Lock Haven, PA
All rights reserved.

ISBN: 9781706397502

>TOURIST

50 TRAVEL TIPS FROM A LOCAL

BOOK DESCRIPTION

Are you excited about planning your next trip? Do you want to try something new? Would you like some guidance from a local? If you answered yes to any of these questions, then this Greater Than a Tourist book is for you. Greater Than a Tourist-Salem, Massachusetts by Danielle Lasher offers the inside scoop on Salem, Massachusetts, America's most notoriously enchanted city. Most travel books tell you how to travel like a tourist. Although there is nothing wrong with that, as part of the Greater Than a Tourist series, this book will give you travel tips from someone who has lived at your next travel destination.

In these pages, you will discover advice that will help you throughout your stay. This book will not tell you exact addresses or store hours but instead will give you excitement and knowledge from a local that you may not find in other smaller print travel books.

Travel like a local. Slow down, stay in one place, and get to know the people and culture. By the time you finish this book, you will be eager and prepared to travel to your next destination.

Inside this travel guide book you will find:

- Insider tips from a local.

- Packing and planning list.

- List of travel questions to ask yourself or others while traveling.

- A place to write your travel bucket list.

OUR STORY

Traveling is a passion of the Greater than a Tourist book series creator. Lisa studied abroad in college, and for their honeymoon Lisa and her husband toured Europe. During her travels to Malta, an older man tried to give her some advice based on his own experience living on the island since he was a young boy. She was not sure if she should talk to the stranger but was interested in his advice. When traveling to some places she was wary to talk to locals because she was afraid that they weren't being genuine. Through her travels, Lisa learned how much locals had to share with tourists. Lisa created the Greater Than a Tourist book series to help connect people with locals. A topic that locals are very passionate about sharing.

TABLE OF CONTENTS

11. The Witch Dungeon Museum is an Unmistakable Icon
12. CinemaSalem — and Bring the Popcorn
13. Jump Out of Your Skin at Count Orlok's Nightmare Gallery
14. Hit Up the Arcade and Casino at Salem Willows
15. All Aboard at the New England Pirate Museum
16. The Grand Halloween Parade is Like No Other

Peaceful Places

17. Set a Serene Scene
18. Take a Stroll Through History on Winter Island
19. Salem Common is Anything But Typical
20. Be One with Nature at Misery Islands
21. No Trip is Complete Without a Psychic Reading

Shop Salem City

22. Haus Witch Has It All
23. Say Cheese!
24. The Oldest Candy Companie in Town
25. Calling All Green Witches
26. Salem Keeps it Spicy
27. Thursdays Downtown Will Raise the Farmers Market Bar
28. Witch City Consignment is the Reigning Champion of Thrift Stores

Eat Like A Local

DEDICATION

This book is dedicated to your inner witch or warlock. May it inspire magic like you've never felt before!

ABOUT THE AUTHOR

Danielle Lasher is a writer, mother, and women's health advocate. Life brought her to Salem many moons ago when her other half was attending law school in Boston. A mere day trip to the haunted city made such an impact that she was home that night apartment-hunting and mentally packing up their house in New Hampshire. Danielle has been in love with the magical north shore city of Salem ever since.

After earning her bachelor's degree in Psychology at Penn State, Danielle made good use of her writing talent and went on to work as a copywriter, providing marketing content on healthcare and drug research to facilities around the globe. But her true love—the world of mothers and babies—was lying in wait. She cut the only career cord she'd ever known and spontaneously changed gears.

Not having looked back, she has since contributed to several online publications, such as BabyGaga, Hot Moms Club, Vaxxter, and the Organic Daily Post. While passionate about women's birthing choices and informed consent, she is also slightly obsessed with city living, travel, antiques, and cooking. When she

3

isn't curating content for the masses or running natural birth and parenting support groups, you can find her refinishing worn-out furniture or binge-watching Bravo. You can catch up with Danielle on her website www.BumpMama.com

HOW TO USE THIS BOOK

The *Greater Than a Tourist* book series was written by someone who has lived in an area for over three months. The goal of this book is to help travelers either dream or experience different locations by providing opinions from a local. The author has made suggestions based on their own experiences. Please check before traveling to the area in case the suggested places are unavailable.

Travel Advisories: As a first step in planning any trip abroad, check the Travel Advisories for your intended destination.
https://travel.state.gov/content/travel/en/
traveladvisories/traveladvisories.html

FROM THE PUBLISHER

Traveling can be one of the most important parts of a person's life. The anticipation and memories that you have are some of the best. As a publisher of the Greater Than a Tourist, as well as the popular *50 Things to Know* book series, we strive to help you learn about new places, spark your imagination, and inspire you. Wherever you are and whatever you do I wish you safe, fun, and inspiring travel.

Lisa Rusczyk Ed. D.
CZYK Publishing

WELCOME TO
> TOURIST

*"Travel is fatal to prejudice,
bigotry, and narrow-mindedness,
and many of our people need it
sorely on these accounts. Broad,
wholesome, charitable views of men
and things cannot be acquired by
vegetating in one little corner of the
earth all one's lifetime."*

– Mark Twain, The Innocents Abroad

A study published in the journal Social Psychology and Personality Science actually confirmed Mark Twain's words to be true. The more people travel, the more open and trusting they are. This highlights a core tenet of who we are as human beings. We mammals are naturally primed for survival — never trusting anyone if we don't have to. But our environment smooths out those rough edges and molds us into better version of ourselves. Thus, the environment we put ourselves in is a critical component of who we become. Salem has definitely shaped the person I've become.

Life in Salem truly is magical. You'll feel it just walking down the street. Those brick-paved paths that were once graced with the footsteps of Nathaniel

11

Hawthorne and Rebecca Nurse lead tourists and locals alike to a myriad of delicious history. Many tourists flock here every year in search of a charming and mystical experience that they can carry with them for the rest of their lives. Believe me, you'll likely find just that. From the underground tunnels and gravesites to the centuries-old legends about what really started the Salem Witch Trials, there is more than meets the eye in this majestic town that should be on everyone's travel bucket list.

If you're looking for a charming seaside New England town that brings a flavor like nothing else you'll see in the northeast, the Witch City is it.

Salem
Massachusetts, USA

Salem Climate

	High	Low
January	37	21
February	39	23
March	45	29
April	56	39
May	66	48
June	75	57
July	81	63
August	80	62
September	73	56
October	62	45
November	52	36
December	42	27

GreaterThanaTourist.com

Temperatures are in Fahrenheit degrees.
Source: NOAA

WHERE TO STAY

1. THE HAWTHORNE HOTEL IS ONE COOL HAUNT

Despite living in Salem, I actually stayed in this hotel with my children when my mom came for a visit. The Hawthorne is very ornate. If you're looking for Victorian-era charm with modern amenities, this is it.

The Hawthorne has that prestigious NYC Plaza Hotel feel inside but on a smaller scale. The hotel is reportedly haunted by the spirit of Bridget Bishop — the first person executed during the 1692 Salem Witch Trials. While the Hawthorne looks like it's been a part of Salem history for centuries, it was actually constructed in 1924. The grand ballroom has been home to many social affairs over the years, but one that stands out is the séance held in 1990 in hopes of summoning Harry Houdini from the afterlife. It was unsuccessful. Womp, womp.

If I was headed to Salem and needed a place to stay, this would be it hands down. The Hawthorne is central to the entire downtown circuit of the city, as well as being near to Pickering Wharf. There is parking on-site and you can't beat an evening cocktail at the in-house Tavern on the Green, where you'll be draped in history on all sides of the polished wood-covered walls.

Breakfast at Nathaniel's is an opportunity worth opting in on, and if they're serving Sunday Brunch, you'd be crazy to skip the Seafood Eggs Benedict — complete with smoked salmon and crab cakes. I say this as a born and raised Maryland girl with pretty high crab cake standards.

2. SALEM WATERFRONT IS FAMILY-FRIENDLY

Not every traveler is bound for a backpack-style adventure, and Salem is by no means a destination limited to adults and couples. The family-friendly hotspot boasts tons of tourism and kid-centric attractions. You might not know it judging from their lodging options though. Apart from the Hawthorne, most of the city is drenched in private rentals, inns and B&B's that tend to cater to smaller or more mature parties.

No need to fret if the Hawthorne is all booked up; there is a more-than-suitable alternative. Many find the Salem Waterfront hotel lends a little bit more of a seacoast feel, which is important to tourists flocking to New England's coastline year-round. The hotel also offers a huge indoor pool, and that's a big plus in this town on a hot summer day. New England isn't always cool during those months. While the hotel is more modern and the décor is akin to what you would find in most cities, the waterfront view more than makes up for it. Make sure to get a room overlooking the harbor.

3. THE AMELIA PAYSON HOUSE IS STEEPED IN ARCHITECTURAL HISTORY

The Amelia Payson House has been through thick and thin with Salem. The double door entrance and Greek Revival architecture just might literally take your breath away. "Amelia's" is the quintessential New England bed and breakfast. If you're looking for seclusion or a splash of romance, this place has it all. Quaint and intimate, it boasts just three bedrooms. So, book well in advance! Fresh fruit, omelets and waffles are just a taste of what you'll enjoy for breakfast while camping out at this B&B.

From the House, you can walk to virtually anything else you desire to see within the city limits. The central location only adds to it being one of the most desirable lodging choices among Salem tourists each year. Recently renovated, Amelia's is five-star lodging in the Witch City.

Wherever your travels lead you, I'd advise sticking to the local territory for lodging. While nearby towns like Lynn and Peabody look to be close by on a map, traffic into and out of Salem — especially during the autumn season — can be dense. Salem is certainly a beautiful city to take in, even through a car window, but I'd recommend doing it on foot and staying within the city.

SO MUCH TO SEE

4. HAVE YOUR PICK AT PICKERING WHARF

No trip to Salem is complete without browsing the shops at Pickering Wharf. This wharf sits overlooking Salem Harbor. You can stand on the same ground that Blackbeard was said to years ago. While you're there, check out The Friendship — a replica ship measuring 171 feet tall that stands as a testament to the Salem East Indiaman Friendship of 1797.

Captured by British opponents in 1812, the original Friendship's reigning tour, which included 15 voyages, came to an end. The modern-day version isn't merely an exterior façade, but the full ship is decked out with details of yesteryear.

While the National Park Service commissioned the building of the replica, many town folk and other volunteers took part in the construction. Lovers of a good sea voyage can attend the annual Salem Maritime Festival each summer where local artisan vendors and historians set up shop on the wharf to

delight locals and tourists alike. I was really
impressed when touring the Friendship of Salem.

5. HEAVY HISTORY HANGS AROUND

Back in 2016, exploration of the Salem Witch Trials
saw quite the boon. Researchers unearthed the
location where 19 innocent people were hanged.
When you're scoping out ornate headstones and wax
museums in Salem, swing by Proctor's Ledge
between Pope Street and Proctor Street to pay your
respects.

Centuries-old documents accounting for eye-witness
testimonies, combined with sonar technology, led
scholars to confirm the location of the hangings.

Although we moved to Salem on a whim after
visiting one day and falling in love with the city, I
wasn't aware until a few years later that there might
be a bigger explanation for my feelings for Witch
City. Research into my family genealogy led me to
discover Rebecca Nurse and her sister Mary Easty —
both executed on suspicion of witchcraft — made

their way into my family tree with their other sis
Sarah Towne Cloyce who was later freed from
imprisonment. I'd be lying if I said these revelations
don't make me wonder about the connection I feel to
Salem.

6. NOT YOUR AVERAGE
CEMETERY

The Old Burying Point Cemetery on Charter Street
kind of takes the cake for me in Salem, if I'm being
honest. Having lived right down the street from it, I
may be biased.

Opened in 1637, this cemetery boasts the perfect
balance of eerie delight you want to feel in a town
like Salem, coupled with the majestic appreciation for
each headstone that has stood the test of time.

The headstones are thick plaques decorated with
angels, skulls and the profiles of children. They stand
as a testament to their time period. The most
spectacular old trees drape themselves over the burial
ground, lending the perfect amount of spook factor as

though it was planned. But it wasn't. This is just how life rolls in Salem.

An onlooker who isn't moved by these grounds and what they represent would be most unusual. While you're walking along the headstones, soak up the creepy but humbling ambiance of the Salem Witch Memorial. Many of Salem's most notable government figures were laid to rest there, from the first burial — Doraty Cromwell — to Mayflower passenger Captain Richard More, to Judge John Hathorne in 1717 with his family buried adjacent to him.

7. THE PEABODY ESSEX MUSEUM DELIGHTS EVERYONE

We're lucky to have a big family who loves to travel and are always on board for visiting us wherever we happen to be living. Their trips to Salem have often included an afternoon spent at the Peabody Essex Museum.

The PEM is far from the average art museum. They don't stick to coloring inside the lines in that place.

From abstract art and Asian exploration to photography and special emphasis on ma pieces, there's no shortage of pieces that make you think gracing the 40,000-square foot space.

If you're like me and you find museums are sometimes hot and stuffy, fear not with the PEM. You can step right outside and across the brick-laden mall to their 5,000-square foot garden sanctuary. Talk about nature art!

If you're really in the mood to travel like a local, check out the PEM during some low-key weeknights when they host immersive tours of 16th and 17th-century homes to discuss their architectural appeal and wonder.

When you leave the PEM, swing by Wicked Good Books on the corner of Essex Street and Derby Square. There is plenty of literature on witchcraft and all things trendy in the hobgoblin world of warlocks, vampires and sorcerers. Still, you'll discover a few diamonds in the rough sifting through the piles of old books, and that book store smell is ever-present.

8. THE WITCH HOUSE BOASTS CLASSIC NEW ENGLAND FLAIR

This house is the epitome of what comes to mind for most of us when we think of a witch's cottage buried deep in the forest — only bigger, and far more haunting. The home originally belonged to Jonathan Corwin, one of the Judges who participated in the Salem Witch Trials and assisted in issuing 19 accused witches to their deaths.

If you're looking for a snapshot that will cement the image of Salem style into your mind forever, this is the place. The architecture is everything one would expect of a well-cared for home from 1700s New England.

The Witch House is on Essex Street, which is a fantastic place to start your travels in Salem. Start at one end and travel through the entire downtown mall and into the historic McIntire District, decked out with its mansard roofs laced with fish scale shingles and manicured lawns with iron gates.

Swing by the Salem Public Library and immerse yourself in the local culture section if the weather turns dreary, as is expected from time to time in New England. Don't worry, the fall foliage looks even brighter after the trees soak up a few raindrops and always pleases the leaf peepers. The Witch House does offer tours, but make sure to check their hours.

9. THE HOUSE OF SEVEN GABLES IS A TRUE MASTERPIECE

While many have read the famed novel by notable author Nathaniel Hawthorne, the House of Seven Gables is a real place with real New England charm throughout every inch of it. Built in 1668 and originally known as the Turner Ingersoll House, it is the prototypical witch's manor in my mind. This house is the image of the home I dream of owning someday, though it won't be this exact one. I wish! The floorplan is more than 8,000 square feet; so, I'll have my work cut out for me with any imitator of it.

Purchased in the early 1900s by the House of Seven Gables Settlement Association, the house was added

to the list of National Historic Landmarks in 2007 —
a few years after my first introduction to it when I fell
in love with its Georgian architectural vibes and
pitch-black coloring. The House was passed down
through three generations of the Turner family before
John Turner III lost his family's fortune over years of
allegedly bad investments and frivolous expenses,
and the house went with it. Many still claim he haunts
the premises, perhaps keeping watch over what he
still believes is still rightfully his.

Across the street, you can finish off your excursion in
the Gables House with a tour of Nathanial
Hawthorne's real birthplace. This house was
relocated from its original location on Union Street in
1958 — that's no small feat! However, it is a
testament to the solid construction of homes from
centuries gone by if you ask me.

10. GALLOWS HILL IS HALLOWED GROUND — SORT OF

Believe it or not, quite a few people make their way
to Salem on occasion and never set foot toward
Gallows Hill. If you know where you're going, then

it's hardly an inconvenience. Gallows Hill is located at the cross-section of Manswell Parkway and Witch Hill Road.

This spot on the map has been a prized destination for years up until recently when it was discovered to be the incorrect location of where the Salem Witch Trial executions were said to have occurred.

Despite knowing that Proctor's Ledge now marks that location, Gallows Hill remains a strong piece of history with many fans of the Witch City interested in scoping it out during their visit.

The location of such was of specific interest to me considered Rebecca Nurse and Mary Easty were both hanged based on the accusation of witchcraft. Legend has it that Rebecca's son Benjamin collected her body after the fact in the middle of the night in order to give her a proper burial on their property.

Historical data notes Benjamin using a waterway and boat to carry this out, but no waterways ever crossed by Gallows Hill — leading one to wonder how the myth of it being the site of the hangings carried on for so long. Perhaps people just wanted a story to cling to in the absence of having any evidence otherwise. Either way, now we know, and Gallows Hill still remains a stop on many travelers to-do lists.

11. THE WITCH DUNGEON MUSEUM IS AN UNMISTAKABLE ICON

Salem is a fringe city to Boston and welcomes people from around the world every year who are hoping to catch of glimpse of the Sanderson Sisters or Freddy Krueger as they walk the streets surrounded by other believers of magic. No trip to the town is complete without spending some time at the Witch Dungeon Museum. The folks running it are the friendliest bunch you'll come across.

During one of my mom's visits, she struggled to choose between which holiday ornament to buy at the gift shop. The last of a certain kind the clerk had in stock was her choice, and she just gave it to my mom free of charge and told her to enjoy her stay in the Witch City. Indeed, you'll find that kind of hospitality here, contrary to popular belief that it's only found in the Deep South.

12. CINEMASALEM — AND BRING THE POPCORN

You haven't lived until you've experienced a horror flick on the small-town silver screen at CinemaSalem. Keep the bar standard in mind that this movie theater is not in competition with luxury cinemas. I saw the 2018 release of Halloween at one of those cinemas; we had our own leather recliners, complete with a pillow and blanket while being served cocktails and filet mignon sliders. I'm not knocking that experience, but going to the movies in Salem is a different experience.

CinemaSalem keeps things a little more traditional, and even though the city has over 40,000 residents with more than half a million visiting each year, the theater emits a more small-town vibe I truly love. This movie house is a Jack-of-all-trades. When it's not filled to the brim with people waiting for the next look at the latest thriller, it may be doubling as an art venue or even a music hall. You'll find it worth your time to follow their website and social media pages to see what's happening during your stay.

13. JUMP OUT OF YOUR SKIN AT COUNT ORLOK'S NIGHTMARE GALLERY

Skip the wax museum; the party's all here. Count Orlok's literally cannot be missed if you're walking around downtown Salem. You'll hear the horrific screams and spooky music amidst the strobe light effects as you walk down Essex taking in the city sights.

Apart from regular events like signings with popular horror film stars, this place brings art to life with replicas of some of the most iconic horror villains we've ever known. Marvel at the full-size models while trying not to be spooked by the Annabelle doll.

When we first moved to Salem, our kids were only what eight and nine. I wouldn't recommend Count Orlok's until a bit older, and we have never been too conservative about horror films with our kids.

14. HIT UP THE ARCADE AND CASINO AT SALEM WILLOWS

Remember that seaside charm I was talking about? You aren't limited to the harbor at Pickering Wharf when visiting Salem. The city boasts its own rocky coastline and beach at its Northeast tip known as the Salem Willows.

You can ooh and ahh at the sights of Dead Horse Beach — a name that caught on as Salemites of the 19th century referenced the beach as being far enough from town to bury a dead horse (no word on whether anyone ever actually did that)!

You can also just opt for picking over the shells at Collins Cove. While you're at the Willows, swing by the arcade and casino. That said, I wouldn't recommend approaching the joint expecting Atlantic City. Think smaller and vintage with batting cages, skeeball and Pac Man. Stop by E.W. Hobbs and grab some popcorn on your way out. The stuff is legendary. You won't regret it.

15. ALL ABOARD AT THE NEW ENGLAND PIRATE MUSEUM

To be honest, I know the history of Salem well. As I mentioned before, Blackbeard and many others set sail and landed in Salem Harbor in years gone by. Still, when I moved to Salem, it left me wondering whether the pirate museum really fit into the town all that well amongst the rest of the attractions.

Does it stand out? Sure, but I wouldn't call it a sore thumb. More so, a place that will pique your curiosity. Take a few minutes to stroll through the museum and engage with the storytellers on the guided tours. This museum will leave you with a different impression of just how dark and dreary a pirate's life could be.

Perhaps it fits well in Salem after all. At the end of the day, this one always hits it out of the park with the kids, and it's a good place to hang out if the weather takes a turn.

16. THE GRAND HALLOWEEN PARADE IS LIKE NO OTHER

If you're lucky enough to be in Salem for Halloween (book these trips a year or more in advance), it'll be an All Hallows' Eve you'll always remember. The candy takeaway isn't all that extreme, but there will certainly be tossing of some goodies to the sides of Salem's historic streets as they are lined with patrons hoping to get an up-close look at the Ghostbuster wagon and decorate hearses.

Local city officials join together with regional boy and girl scout troops, as well as schoolchildren and more, getting all decked out for what is arguably one of the best Halloween parades in the world. Okay, maybe I'm partial, but it's seriously impressive. There's nowhere else I'd rather be on Halloween night.

PEACEFUL PLACES

17. SET A SERENE SCENE

After all that skipping about town, you might be in need a minute to just take it all in. Forest River Park is an ideal place to do it.

Something that was new to me upon moving to Salem was the concrete slide. I would never have known it was one if I hadn't been told such. Bring a piece of cardboard and let the kids and adults enjoy a little downtime in this peaceful park with its harbor views. I'm not kidding; don't knock the concrete slide until you try it. Kids love this one during snowstorms, too.

18. TAKE A STROLL THROUGH HISTORY ON WINTER ISLAND

If every place in town is booked and you're dead set on seeing Salem anyway, the campgrounds at Winter Island park just might be your ticket to this ghostly paradise.

Winter Island is actually the closest campground to the state's Beantown capital. A well-kept secret, many RV-ers have no idea there is space for them in Salem.

Winter Island Light, also known as the Fort Pickering Lighthouse is a smaller lighthouse off the coast of the harbor. There since construction in 1871, the lighthouse worked in conjunction with several other lighthouses in the area to direct ships into the harbor. The alternative name stems from defense fort that exists across from it where troops could seek cover during the Civil War.

19. SALEM COMMON IS ANYTHING BUT TYPICAL

If you look up a picture of Salem Common, you might be wondering what's so magical about it. That's because the pictures taken of the Common are of just that — the Common. The real magic of this plot of land starts from inside it, looking outward.

If you have time to pick up lunch from Longboard's, pack it up and head north to the friendly gazebo at the Common's center. Whether it's a beautiful warm-weather day or it's draped in Christmas lights with a tree, the view is breathtaking.

From inside the Common, you get to take in the panoramic view of what Salem was so many years ago in the 19th century. Graced with brick mansions and architectural delights from days gone by, these homes were built for some of the wealthiest politicians and legislators Salem ever knew. Many of the homes are still adorned with the names of their original owners.

The 1811 House that belonged to Joseph Story, a United States Supreme Court Associate Justice, is one of my favorites with its grand federal stature and portico. They really don't make them like this anymore. If you love English architecture and are like me, wishing America had more of it, you'll adore every street in Salem.

20. BE ONE WITH NATURE AT MISERY ISLANDS

It sounds like the kind of name for an island you'd expect from a city like Salem, right? It was allegedly named such after shipbuilder Robert Moulton found himself stranded on the island in the 1620s during a Winter storm, leading to a nickname of "Moulton's Misery."

Summer is the best time of year to get a full tour of the islands in because you can only get to Little Misery Island by sloshing through a shallow channel between it and Great Misery Island, which is only accessible by boat.

This is also only advisable at low tide, and seriously, don't go alone. Back in the early 1900s, the Islands were in their heyday boasting tennis courts, a saltwater pool and a golf course, clubhouse and more. The islands thrived until a brush fire claimed many of the cottages as well as a Casino hotel.

The island still holds the 12 original granite pillars that once held a water tower. A 274-foot steamboat named City of Rockland was scuttled on the rocky coastline of the island in 1923 and its remnants remain there today for you to gaze upon. Wear comfy shoes and enjoy the nature trails while you're there.

21. NO TRIP IS COMPLETE WITHOUT A PSYCHIC READING

It's not everyone's thing. Some people are adamantly against fortune-telling and psychic abilities, but if you're not in that camp, head over to Magika for the experience of a lifetime.

A Sicilian Strega witch, High Priestess Lori Bruno knows the craft well. Most who have been to a reading with her will tell you she doesn't hold back. In other words, make sure you're ready to hear anything and hear from anyone.

SHOP SALEM CITY

22. HAUS WITCH HAS IT ALL

When you're feeling well-rested, hit up Haus Witch for vintage vibes that you can only find in the Witch City. The shop's décor options are tailored to the modern-day witch. From wall hangings and geometrical patterns you thought only existed on Pinterest, to the essential oil-infused cleaning products for kitchen witches to clean up nice, this place hits the witchery feel out of the park.

Scope them out before heading to Salem and consider scheduling your trip around one of their workshops, which can school you on everything from herbal remedies to crafting spells.

23. SAY CHEESE!

Listen, every tourist town may check this one off the list, but know that every tourist town is not this close to Vermont. Wisconsin has nothin' on New England,

and the Cheese Shop of Salem is where it's at. If you're going to miss the weekly Farmer's Market, I highly suggest swinging by this local shop on Lafayette Street and sample some of the most decadent cheeses you'll find in the region.

The Cheese Shop of Salem isn't just limited to dairy though; they're serving up perfectly paired bottles of vino, too! If you're hosting a group trip — think: girl's weekend — in Salem, this is the prime destination for grabbing a cheese platter and some wine to settle in on your first night in town.

Taking things another impressive step forward, if you just can't part with the Vacherousse d'Argental or find yourself longing for the bold flavor of the Prairie Breeze Cheddar when you get home, this cheese shop ships their goods right to your door! Check out their monthly wine and cheese club while you're at it. This shop trumps anything the mainstream wine and cheese clubs have going on.

24. THE OLDEST CANDY COMPANIE IN TOWN

This slice of Salem history is particularly interesting because it's not only the oldest candy company in Salem but the oldest in the United States. The Ye Olde Pepper Candy Companie opened in 1806.

If you've never indulged in a blackjack or a Salem gibralter, you don't know what you're missing. Hoarding the goodies this place has to offer all to myself would be wrong.

Their fudge gives my grandmother's fair competition, and their saltwater taffy gives the rest of the New England coastline a run for their money, too.

The candy shop's exterior is dressed to the nines in New England architecture, and the smell of sugary sweetness smacks you in the face when you open the door in the best possible way. There's nothing better to walk into and feel the literal warm welcome if you're visiting during the chillier months of the year.

25. CALLING ALL GREEN WITCHES

If you're new to witching and drawn to the more natural and earthy elements like herbalism, Artemisia Botanicals can fix you up and send you on your way as a more educated and informed witch in no time.

Their Green Witch School will take you from newbie to a wild witch of wellness all while helping you learn to appreciate the many facets of the craft that may benefit you.

I picked up one of my favorite journals from Artemisia Botanicals and they're my go-to for light-safe tincture bottles for my most-loved herbal remedies.

26. SALEM KEEPS IT SPICY

This place is not your average spice shop. For starters, it's owned by the ever so eclectic David Bowie. No, not that David Bowie (may he rest in peace). But a David Bowie nonetheless who knows his profession well.

This tasty spice shop brings you individual spices and tasty blends from around the world to delight your senses. If you're a fan of pickled beets or eggs, don't leave without a pack of their peppercorns and caraway seeds; they're my absolute favorite.

27. THURSDAYS DOWNTOWN WILL RAISE THE FARMERS MARKET BAR

This is one of my favorite travel tips, and it's not restricted to Salem. When I'm off seeing the world, taking in local Farmers Markets is high on my list. Not only am I a major foodie who loves to sample local goods, but it's the ideal place to find yourself immersed in local culture, too.

This is truly where the locals are. In Salem, you'll find them picking up the best dinner ingredients their region has to offer while hob-knobbing with farmers from Maine to Mass to New Hampshire and more.

Need some obscure aged cheddar from the mountains of Vermont? Perhaps you're dying to sample a little local honey—the Salem Farmers Market is your spot.

While Salem is a dense and somewhat smaller city, it's Farmers Market is anything but. Sprawled out across Derby Square in front of the old Town Hall, it brings not just produce but cheeses, handmade pastas, meats, freshly baked breads, desserts and more to

Salemites each week from June to October with two bonus markets in the Winter season.

If you were raised South of the Mason-Dixon line like me, snatch up the green tomatoes to take home and fry up; you won't find them anywhere else in the Witch City. P.S. Do not skip the samples.

28. WITCH CITY CONSIGNMENT IS THE REIGNING CHAMPION OF THRIFT STORES

Truth be told, thrifting wasn't really a hobby of mine until I moved to Salem; now it's a habit I cannot seem to break. Not that I'm trying very hard. Whether you're just killing time on a Saturday afternoon, looking for a piece to rehab and flip, or wanting to add a little more classic New England charm to your home, you won't find a better deal in this region.

I've stumbled upon some of my favorite records in this place, as well as some of the most awe-inspiring pieces I've ever seen. For example, I spent months oohing and ahhing at an old pair of doors that once graced the entrance to a New England church. They must've been ten feet high. I had no purpose for them, but boy do I still wish I had! Check it out; you'll love it!

EAT LIKE A LOCAL

29. DUBE'S SEAFOOD IS ANYTHING BUT DUBIOUS

By now, you're probably working up an appetite. While New England isn't always known for their culinary creations (I blame the English and their frugality on salt), Salem is a surefire exception.

If you're looking for a taste of Salem cuisine, you'll find it at Dube's. This seafood joint is the kind of place that even those with a Southern accent (what people in Salem think I have but I don't hear it) are treated like locals.

The food comes to you fresh from the fryer — assuming you're ordering their highly praised fried whole belly clams, that is. Dube's is not a fancy place. Feel free to dress comfortably and enjoy a pint with your seafood platter.

30. A LITTLE MEXICO IN NEW ENGLAND

Howling Wolf Taqueria is the best place in town for a quick bite of Mexican flavor. This fiery joint is also home to one of my absolute favorite desserts: fried ice cream. If you're new to the dish, I suggest starting with dessert. Otherwise, dinner might be filling as you rush to clear every bit of chipotle-cilantro white sauce from your plate. No excuses! Get the ice cream; it'll change your life.

31. GO GREEK

No stroll down the historic mall is complete without two things: someone is out there playing music, and the rest of us are listening along while chowing down on pierogis from the Polonus Euro Deli. This is where you can order the pierogis that will be the end of the pierogi as you ever knew it. Ask for extra servings of the tart sour cream.

32. LITTLE ITALY

Table for two? This place boasts some seriously tight quarters. I'm not sure they can hold more than 40 diners, if that. Still, if you're craving Italian, there's really nowhere else in town I'd recommend.

Bella Verona sits on Essex Street, just off of Hawthorne and adjacent to the Hawthorne Hotel. Tucked away like a cozy European restaurant with its hallmark black and white striped awning, it is definitely the cutest eatery in the city.

If you're lucky, you can score the front window seat and watch the passersby enjoying their time in this city full of charm. Order the Linguini Alle Delicie Del Mare if you love a good pasta and seafood mixture. Bella Verona is the perfect blend of Italy meets the New England seacoast.

33. A SLICE OF SALEM

Back in the summer of 2012 when we had just moved to Salem, the Flying Saucer Pizza Company set up shop downtown. This grand opening was history in the making and no one knew it yet.

As you might have gleaned from its name, this pie palace has a strong Sci-Fi theme. Once you get your travel dates on the books, scope out their events page to see if any of their famed events are going on, like their Stranger Things themed brunch.

Pizza toppings are a personal choice, and I respect that, but if Salem makes you feel as wild and free as the rest of us, Poison Ivy pizza with the Piranha cocktail. Lots of vegan and veggie options here!

34. BOSTON HOT COMPANY

This is definitely a standing

favorite of our kids'. Parents love it because the Boston Hot Dog Company is more like a fancy street cart than a restaurant. Walk right up, place your order, and in minutes, you're off with Salem Trolley Dog — complete with baked beans, cheddar cheese, tomato, red onion, and lettuce — in hand. This is the perfect to-go food since you won't find many drive-thrus in Salem proper. Of course, if you're not the adventurous type that likes piles of hot dog toppings, they can do it your way, too; just ask for the Sinatra dog.

35. YOU MUST STOP AT RED'S SANDWICH SHOP

Part of the charm of Salem's downtown mall is the magical places you'll find when turning the corner onto Central Street, which really feels more like a secret alley you've stumbled upon in London.

Speaking of which, Red's Sandwich Shop is actually housed in the historic London Coffee House building that dates back to the late 1600s. You know those places that you can rely on for coffee that is always fresh and stacks of pancakes that just keep coming? Expect that.

Also expect a diner vibe inside, which I'll admit can throw you off based on the building's exterior, but the food is well worth it.

36. KENS KICKIN' CHICKEN PIES ARE A TASTE OF THE SOUTH

If you've rented a house and have access to an oven, this is a must to add to your list. Yes, I'm actually suggesting you eat dinner in while in Salem. Just once!

Marvel at the glorious Victorian-era homes while on your way to North Street for Ken's Kickin' Chicken. If you're pining for an easy side dish that doesn't require any prep, everything from the downtown Steve's Market to Whole Foods in nearby Swampscott are within your reach.

37. THE GULU-GULU CAFE

While Mr. Crepe might steal your attention when you're researching all the tasty snacks Salem has to offer, the best crepes in town can actually be found at the Gulu-Gulu Café. Don't worry, this isn't just some random dessert bar. You can swing by here for breakfast with a cup of mud, or have lunch in a wrap with a great salad on the side, or bowl of goulash.

Those crepes take the cake though! They range from the most savory to the most sweet. Word to the wise: Leave room for dessert! The same extraordinary food connoisseurs behind the Flying Saucer Pizza Company are actually those behind the Gulu, too.

38. FOR HIGH-END EATS, HEAD TO FINZ

In the heart of Pickering Wharf sits one of my favorite Salem restaurants to date. What should you have? Raw oysters are a must on my list to get things started, and their bar has never disappointed me, whether picking from what's on tap or ordering a specifically curated cocktail.

For dinner, it's usually surf 'n turf for me. Both are always cooked perfectly. The interior charm is akin to any high-end, nautical-themed restaurant. The blue light fish tank is seriously impressive and will put other seafood restaurants to shame.

39. SALEM IS SO SWEET

I've yet to have a family member or friend visit Salem that I didn't insist they go to Maria's Sweet Somethings. When we first moved to Salem, we had a pretty nice apartment downtown right in the center of it all above what is now the Derby Restaurant. Maria's sits adjacent to the rear of that building and promises to leave its mark on you. Her hot chocolate fudge sauce is something no other ice cream shop has beaten on my list of food favorites — and I've done my due diligence in ice cream shopping across the states. If you're in town for the So Sweet Chocolate and Ice Sculpture Festival, Maria's display is usually pretty remarkable.

NORTH SHORE NIGHTLIFE

40. LOBSTER SHANTY TO GET WILD WITH THE LOCALS

If you're in the mood for a pint, the Lobster Shanty is slinging beers all night long. Alright, not really all night long, but don't assume every New England town rolls up the sidewalks at dusk.

Salem is a college town through and through. The party scene is alive and well if that's what you're about, and Lobster Shanty is one place you can find a mixture of locals of all ages with a few tourists like yourself sprinkled in.

The Shanty's central downtown location across from the old Town Hall makes for a quiet outdoor seating arrangement when the weather allows. If you're here for the Winter season, sit inside and hope for a storm. You just might see snow-lovers like myself slipping around town in snowshoes or even skis!

41. THE DERBY RESTAURANT

Once upon a time, this place was called the Tavern in the Square — commonly referenced by locals as, ahem, TITS. People ask me to this day if it bothered me to live above the Tavern bar. Sure, the bikers were loud at times, but honestly, no one is louder than the band of girls in heels at 1 AM who meet outside to discuss the guys waiting inside that they just met.

Still, the conversations were humorous, and it's not eavesdropping when I'm on my sofa and they're just that loud. Case in point, no one is going to shush you around here. Downtown Salem is a free-for-all. Embrace it for what it is and enjoy it!

42. IT'S ALWAYS CIDER SEASON IN SALEM

Stop along Jackson Street for a tasting of all Far From the Tree Hard Cider has to offer. From the most out-there of flavors like Strawberry Basil to the more traditional Scarecrow that boasts the seasonal apple spice flavors all fall-lovers long for, to the Salem-centric Ectoplasm flavor derived from jalapenos, bell peppers and kiwi, you'll be in for a surprise. And yes, it's totally Slimer-colored.

Seriously, don't knock it till you try it. The cider business is owned by a married couple who brought their dream of sharing their love of fermenting apples for grown-ups to reality right here in Salem.

43. THE LOCAL WATERING HOLE

You know that hole-in-the-wall place that might feel a little dark and dank and is almost fit for a TV-movie? Every town has one. This is Salem's. Major's is the premiere dive bar for Salemites and visitors alike, but you'll truly find more locals here.

If you're missing the thrill of a big win playing Keno or craving wings and chili, Major's is a must on the list. This place is an institution around here, having been around for more than four decades. Bring your quarters for the jukebox!

44. A NOTCH ABOVE

While not ideal for the latest of late nights, Notch Brewing is a great pub for dinnertime and post-meal chatter with the locals at the bar. Aptly named for the nick one makes to keep record of how many brews they've had, it's easy to lose track downing this pub's pints.

Notch is particularly unique because it's the first brewery in America is focus solely on session beers, which are beers with a lower alcohol content; Notch's are 4.5% and below. Their biergarten is one of the best spots in town for year-round sipping with a waterside view.

45. BIT BY BIT

It sounds like your standard bar, but Bit By Bit is anything but average. That's because it's not just a bar, and it's not just a bar with a restaurant, but a bar with a restaurant and an arcade.

Finally! Rejoice with me that grown-ups like us can get down with Donkey Kong, Ms. Pac-Man and Mortal Kombat while chowing down on our favorite bar foods and brewskies. Adulthood has arrived!

The building's architecture alone — complete with cupolas more than a century old — is worth marveling over, but the details from its prime years as the Old Salem Jail are satisfyingly creepy. So is knowing Albert DeSalvo, more often known as the Boston Strangler, was once housed there. Try to keep that off your mind while becoming the next reigning pinball champ of Salem.

46. THE TUNNELS

I include this in nightlife because although you can tour the underground sector of Salem during the daylight hours, nighttime adds a certain element that you'll definitely feel is missing when the sun is shining.

If you're going to go visit a town with a whole other network of streets beneath it, exploring them better be high on your list of things to check out. The Tunnels are far from dreary and dank because Salem's tourism industry has taken hold and kept them up for visitors like yourself.

Rumor has it that many of the judges and notable figures of years gone by in Salem used to utilize the tunnels to sneak out of their homes at night to see their mistresses.

Getting a bit darker, legends have been passed on for years in Salem that many slaves were buried in the tunnels, specifically in the tunnel running out from the Daniel Low building. This was allegedly an intentional choice a the time since proper burials would've hindered the freedom of other runaway slaves. Some also claim the head of a witch was buried under the city somewhere. Enter if you dare.

GET OUT OF TOWN

47. BASKING IN BEVERLY

If you're willing to travel a little bit outside of the downtown limits, you'll find more to love on that the mainstream travel sites won't mention. Take a stroll down Lafayette Street from Derby Street. As you exit downtown, you'll notice the apartment builders fade and the grand old Victorian mansions start springing up.

In nearby Beverly, there are some charming seaside homes just off of Cabot Street. The Cityside Diner makes the best pancakes in the area and you can serve your whole family for dirt cheap.

48. MAKE ROOM FOR MARBLEHEAD

In the other direction, Marblehead, Massachusetts is the elite edge of Salem. This neighboring town is the upper crust of this sect of the North Shore and boasts some of the most jaw-dropping homes you'll see during your stay. While it's a much smaller town, there is still plenty to see.

Feeling artsy? The King Hooper Mansion boasts some of the most spectacular artwork on the seashore. The nearby Marblehead Museum, in the Jeremiah Lee Mansion, houses a beautiful display of art and history on the region. Carve out time to really immerse yourself in their Civil War artifacts.

It might sound funny, but I strongly recommend stopping by the Old Hill burial ground before you scoot back over to Salem. This place is one of the most stunning cemeteries I've ever spent time in as it overlooks the Atlantic Ocean and part of the town.

49. ROUTE 1 PAVES THE WAY

From Florida up to Maine, Route 1 extends itself across a stretch of the Eastern seaboard that is hard to let go of once you've seen it. But, speaking as an Eastern shore gypsy, the Northeast sect is by far the most breathtaking. I always tell people the seacoast of New England really does feel like you're living on the set of a movie. Who wouldn't want that?

While bigger, more well-known towns like Cape Cod and Martha's Vineyard certainly have their appeal, I recommend making time for the rest of New England's coastline.

I've have had the luxury of living up and down much of the shore. From Salem, you'll want to head north and stop in first in Newburyport. This is a great place to spend some serious money on staples pieces for your home. No worries, business owners in Mass know how to ship.

The next stop is Portsmouth, New Hampshire, which borders Kittery, Maine. The outlets in Kittery are known to attract people far and wide. Even Canadians make their way down to shop. Portsmouth's downtown is full of delicious restaurants. The charcuterie board at the Carriage House is unforgettable.

The third stop on your route ought to be York, Maine. The Sand Dollar Bar and Grille has the best views in town from their deck on the second story of the Atlantic House Inn. Down the strip, you'll find The Goldenrod. You'll know it from the flashy lights and the huge taffy pulling machine in the window prepping your saltwater delights. This is a big hit with the kids. Inside, their old-fashioned soda fountain is unlike anything else you'll see on the shores of Maine.

Yes, if you grew up south of Jersey, you'll probably think the ocean feels quite chilly even in the August heat, but the beaches are still beautiful with their mix of smooth sand and rocky coastline.

If you're still longing to see more — as you should be — then head straight up "The One," as the locals call it. If towns like Ogunquit and Wells pique your interest, stop and soak up their quaint shops or play a round of putt-putt. Don't languish for too long though. One of my favorite places in the nation lies just a smidgen further north — Kennebunkport.

If you're looking for quintessential New England like you see in the movies, Kennebunkport is it! I was blessed to have lived there many moons ago. The downtown area known as Dock Square is sure to cement itself in your memories. Swing by Alisson's Restaurant for trivia and tapas before heading to Federal Jacks for local brew and a brownie.

If you're really into road-tripping like I am, you'll finish the last leg of your trip by hightailing it to Portland, Maine. The cobblestone streets of the historic city's downtown tell a story you'll always remember — so long as you don't have one too many at Ri Ra's or the Thirsty Pig. The best part? No need to trek back to Boston for a flight. The Portland International Jetport can hook you up and get you on your way.

50. BOSTON

There is certainly no shortage of information about hot spots to visit in Boston. Full of landmarks, you're sure to stumble upon history with every step. Being a tourist in Beantown is fun — scoping out the stairs to Cheers as they disappear into the pavement, and marveling at the Freedom Trail. Still, Boston has more to offer than you're going to find on any travel website.

St. Leonard's Roman Catholic Church is one of the most decadent and ornate religious sanctuaries I've ever laid eyes on in the states. I'm not Catholic, but it made me want to be.

In the North End, step inside of Modern Pastry and try not to buy everything. Seriously, I dare you. Pizelles, Florentines, Pignoli cookies and all things Italian pastry will fill your belly fast. Save room, because JM Curley's duck poutine and pressed Cubano sandwich are next if you're seeking real flavor in the city. Drinks at Eastern Standard are a must if you want to hob-knob with the locals. Try the Augusta cocktail.

BONUS TIP 1: DANVERS: THE REAL SALEM

Alas, we get down to the truth. The Salem Witch Trials, the city's primary claim to unfortunate fame, did not actually occur in the city you will walk about. The Trials occurred in the neighboring town of Danvers, which is a quick 10-minute car ride from Salem.

Of particular interest to me has always been Danvers State Hospital. Converted into apartments in 2006, much of its architecture remains the same in true New England fashion. Many claim it is haunted by the spirits of tortured souls who lost their lives at the facility during its operation from 1878 to the 1960s.

Before its proper real estate upgrade, the movie Session 9 was filmed there and showcases the darkness and morbidity the manor-like estate held. If I hadn't known about the history of the film location, I likely would rate it lower, but I'm biased and have rose-colored glasses when it comes to all things New England history.

Extra Extra!

BONUS TIP 2: PARKING APLENTY

Parking your ride is pretty feasible. Expect more difficulty in September and October, but overall there is plenty of street and lot parking, as well as a handful of parking garages.

BONUS TIP 3: ALTERNATIVES TO DRIVING

In Massachusetts, the public transit system is known as "the T." You can walk to and take the T from Salem to other hot spots like Boston or Newburyport in roughly a half-hour without the headache of metro area traffic.

BONUS TIP 4: THE SALEM TROLLEY

This sweet ride any time of the year. The sweet ride comes out for a sneak peek in the summertime but makes most of its joyrides during the Halloween and Christmas holiday seasons. You can tour the city from it because buses just can't hold a candle to the town trolley.

BONUS TIP 5: SAFETY FIRST

Don't worry too much about staying out late in Salem. The only sketchy part of town is marked on maps as "The Point" and that's still pretty mild. The crime rates are fairly low downtown and tourists aren't often the subject of such anyway. Furthermore, the streets of the downtown mall and surrounding are all lit up with sparkling lights year-round. This adds a certain element of charm that I admit has made me feel other cities are lacking now.

BONUS TIP 6: BUDGET BITES

Plan your meals if you aren't prepared to eat on the fly and need budget-friendly options. While there are oodles of restaurants in Salem to suit all wallets and taste buds, you won't find much in the way of fast food joints in the immediate vicinity. This is intentional. We promise, it only adds to the charm not to have any golden arches in the middle of your downtown historic mall.

69

BONUS TIP 7: TAKE OFF

The closest airport is, fortunately, a major one. Boston Logan International Airport can get you where you need to go.

Overall, Salem is very family-friendly, but do expect some lingering horror flick villains to lurk around Orlok's place, and you might bump into a zombie or two on the street. Prepare your little ones if this is of concern, but Salem workers are a pretty smart bunch. They're not new to the trade and no one is going out of their way to terrify your toddler.

TOP REASONS TO BOOK THIS TRIP

The rocky coastline: This is like something right out of a Stephen King novel. You won't find beaches like this on the rest of the seaboard moving South.

Halloween: October is truly magickal. If you can come during the spookiest time of year, I highly recommend it. The energy in Salem around Halloween is like no other. Everyone is here for the same beloved reason and you can really feel it. Halloween in Salem is the biggest holiday party you'll ever attend. If you're not totally down with the crowds of the Halloween season, Salem is still a fantastic option during other parts of the year. Most of the main attractions remain open. The bronze statue of Elizabeth Montgomery — otherwise known as Samantha Stephens of Bewitched — is still watching over the town from the end of the Essex Street Pedestrian Mall.

Local Flavor: Expect to run into a warlock, pilgrim or Michael Myers when you're grabbing your morning brew at Front Street Coffee House. That's how folks roll in Salem.

71

The Architecture: Salem's scenery takes you back centuries and really showcases the pride involved in our ancestor's efforts to settle and build the city of Salem.

History: This isn't a day at a museum reading about names you've never heard and places you never cared to go. Salem is the perfect mixture of history and pop culture. This is what makes it the ideal trip for anyone, from ancestry buffs like myself who just have to know where their 10x great grandfather lived, to couples looking for a weekend getaway like no other, to families wanting a fun trip for their kids they'll always hold close.

New England Culture: It's unlike anything else you'll find in the states and boasts a far more European than American vibe in some areas.

OTHER RESOURCES:

https://www.salem.org/

https://www.salem.org/map-of-salem/

https://hauntedhappenings.org/wp-content/uploads/2018/06/Map-of-Downtown-Salem-MA.pdf

PACKING AND PLANNING TIPS

A Week before Leaving

- Arrange for someone to take care of pets and water plants.

- Email and Print important Documents.

- Get Visa and vaccines if needed.

- Check for travel warnings.

- Stop mail and newspaper.

- Notify Credit Card companies where you are going.

- Passports and photo identification is up to date.

- Pay bills.

- Copy important items and download travel Apps.

- Start collecting small bills for tips.

- Have post office hold mail while you are away.

- Check weather for the week.

- Car inspected, oil is changed, and tires have the correct pressure.

- Check airline luggage restrictions.

- Download Apps needed for your trip.

Right Before Leaving

- Contact bank and credit cards to tell them your location.

- Clean out refrigerator.

- Empty garbage cans.

- Lock windows.

- Make sure you have the proper identification with you.

- Bring cash for tips.

- Remember travel documents.

- Lock door behind you.

- Remember wallet.

- Unplug items in house and pack chargers.

- Change your thermostat settings.

- Charge electronics, and prepare camera memory cards.

READ OTHER
GREATER THAN A TOURIST
BOOKS

Greater Than a Tourist- Geneva Switzerland: 50 Travel Tips from a Local by Amalia Kartika

Greater Than a Tourist- St. Croix US Birgin Islands USA: 50 Travel Tips from a Local by Tracy Birdsall

Greater Than a Tourist- San Juan Puerto Rico: 50 Travel Tips from a Local by Melissa Tait

Greater Than a Tourist – Lake George Area New York USA: 50 Travel Tips from a Local by Janine Hirschklau

Greater Than a Tourist – Monterey California United States: 50 Travel Tips from a Local by Katie Begley

Greater Than a Tourist – Chanai Crete Greece: 50 Travel Tips from a Local by Dimitra Papagrigoraki

Greater Than a Tourist – The Garden Route Western Cape Province South Africa: 50 Travel Tips from a Local by Li-Anne McGregor van Aardt

Greater Than a Tourist – Sevilla Andalusia Spain: 50 Travel Tips from a Local by Gabi Gazon

Children's Book: *Charlie the Cavalier Travels the World* by Lisa Rusczyk Ed. D.

> TOURIST

Follow us on Instagram for beautiful travel images:
http://Instagram.com/GreaterThanATourist

Follow *Greater Than a Tourist* on Amazon.

>Tourist Podcast

>T Website

>T Youtube

>T Facebook

>T TikTok

>T Goodreads

>T Amazon

>T Mailing List

>T Pinterest

>T Instagram

>T Twitter

>T SoundCloud

>T LinkedIn

>T Map

> TOURIST

At *Greater Than a Tourist*, we love to share travel tips with you. How did we do? What guidance do you have for how we can give you better advice for your next trip? Please send your feedback to GreaterThanaTourist@gmail.com as we continue to improve the series. We appreciate your constructive feedback. Thank you.

METRIC CONVERSIONS

TEMPERATURE

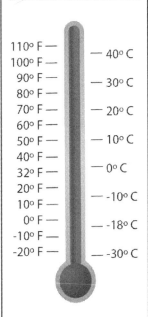

110° F —	— 40° C
100° F —	
90° F —	— 30° C
80° F —	
70° F —	— 20° C
60° F —	
50° F —	— 10° C
40° F —	
32° F —	— 0° C
20° F —	
10° F —	— -10° C
0° F —	
-10° F —	— -18° C
-20° F —	— -30° C

To convert F to C:

Subtract 32, and then multiply by 5/9 or .5555.

To Convert C to F:

Multiply by 1.8 and then add 32.

32F = 0C

LIQUID VOLUME

To Convert:..................Multiply by
U.S. Gallons to Liters................ 3.8
U.S. Liters to Gallons 26
Imperial Gallons to U.S. Gallons 1.2
Imperial Gallons to Liters....... 4.55
Liters to Imperial Gallons 22
1 Liter = .26 U.S. Gallon
1 U.S. Gallon = 3.8 Liters

DISTANCE

To convert ....Multiply by
Inches to Centimeters 2.54
Centimeters to Inches 39
Feet to Meters...................... .3
Meters to Feet 3.28
Yards to Meters 91
Meters to Yards 1.09
Miles to Kilometers 1.61
Kilometers to Miles............. .62
1 Mile = 1.6 km
1 km = .62 Miles

WEIGHT

1 Ounce = .28 Grams
1 Pound = .4555 Kilograms
1 Gram = .04 Ounce
1 Kilogram = 2.2 Pounds

83

TRAVEL QUESTIONS

- Do you bring presents home to family or friends after a vacation?

- Do you get motion sick?

- Do you have a favorite billboard?

- Do you know what to do if there is a flat tire?

- Do you like a sun roof open?

- Do you like to eat in the car?

- Do you like to wear sun glasses in the car?

- Do you like toppings on your ice cream?

- Do you use public bathrooms?

- Did you bring a cell phone and does it have power?

- Do you have a form of identification with you?

- Have you ever been pulled over by a cop?

- Have you ever given money to a stranger on a road trip?

- Have you ever taken a road trip with animals?

- Have you ever gone on a vacation alone?

- Have you ever run out of gas?

- If you could move to any place in the world, where would it be?

- If you could travel anywhere in the world, where would you travel?

- If you could travel in any vehicle, which one would it be?

- If you had three things to wish for from a magic genie, what would they be?

- If you have a driver's license, how many times did it take you to pass the test?

- What are you the most afraid of on vacation?

- What do you want to get away from the most when you are on vacation?

- What foods smell bad to you?

- What item do you bring on ever trip with you away from home?

- What makes you sleepy?

- What song would you love to hear on the radio when you're cruising on the highway?

- What travel job would you want the least?

- What will you miss most while you are away from home?

- What is something you always wanted to try?

- What is the best road side attraction that you ever saw?

- What is the farthest distance you ever biked?

- What is the farthest distance you ever walked?

- What is the weirdest thing you needed to buy while on vacation?

- What is your favorite candy?

- What is your favorite color car?

- What is your favorite family vacation?

- What is your favorite food?

- What is your favorite gas station drink or food?

- What is your favorite license plate design?

- What is your favorite restaurant?

- What is your favorite smell?

- What is your favorite song?

- What is your favorite sound that nature makes?

- What is your favorite thing to bring home from a vacation?

- What is your favorite vacation with friends?

- What is your favorite way to relax?

- Where is the farthest place you ever traveled in a car?

- Where is the farthest place you ever went North, South, East and West?

- Where is your favorite place in the world?

- Who is your favorite singer?

- Who taught you how to drive?

- Who will you miss the most while you are away?

- Who if the first person you will contact when you get to your destination?

- Who brought you on your first vacation?

- Who likes to travel the most in your life?

- Would you rather be hot or cold?

- Would you rather drive above, below, or at the speed limited?

- Would you rather drive on a highway or a back road?

- Would you rather go on a train or a boat?

- Would you rather go to the beach or the woods?

NOTES

Made in the USA
Columbia, SC
07 October 2022

69086840R00062